WHITEWATER SPORT

WHITEWATER SPORT

William Bixby

David McKay Company, Inc.
New York

Copyright © 1978 by William Bixby

All rights reserved, including the right to reproduce this book, or parts thereof, in any form, except for the inclusion of brief quotations in a review.

Library of Congress Cataloging in Publication Data

Bixby, William.
   Whitewater sport.

   SUMMARY: An illustrated introduction to whitewater boating including a discussion of different kinds of rivers, various types of craft, training, safety, and required equipment for the sport.
    1. White-water canoeing—Juvenile literature.
[1. White-water canoeing.   2. Canoes and canoeing]
I. Title.
GV788.B58   797.1'22   78-5206
ISBN 0-679-21050-4

10 9 8 7 6 5 4 3 2 1
Manufactured in the United States of America

Acknowledgements

The author would like to thank Walley and Lynn Williams of Belmont, Massachusetts, for their advice and help throughout the writing of this book. The author also wishes to thank Mrs. George Wendt of OARS (Outdoor Adventure River Specialists), Angels Camp, California, for photographic assistance.

Illustration Credits

Photographs on pages viii, 3, 5, 25, 29, 31, 36, 40, 43, 49, and 53 by Lynn Williams; on pages 19 and 22 by Joseph Bauer, and on page 12 by Donald A. Bedard. Photographs and drawings reproduced on pages 33, 44, and 45, courtesy of Hyperform, Hingham, Massachusetts. The photograph on page 9 was supplied by The National Archives (Photo number 80-G-664442). Photograph on page 13 by John Ross.

Contents

Whitewater: The New Sport   1
Where the Boats Come From   6
Whitewater High   11
Where Whitewater Runs   20
Today's Whitewater Craft   28
Training, Safety, and Equipment   38
Racing   48

A one-man, closed-deck canoe (C-1) punches through a wave in a wildwater race, a downriver event where speed alone is the goal.

1 / *Whitewater: The New Sport*

THE SMALL VILLAGE of North River, New York, ordinarily is a quiet town. But every year, on the first weekend in May, the 250 villagers are host to about 500 whitewater canoeists and kayakers who gather along the banks of the Hudson River. They are there for the Hudson River Whitewater Derby. The Derby has been run for more than twenty years, but only recently has it attracted so many whitewater participants. The spectators number 25,000. North River gets very crowded at Derby Time.

The Hudson is a beautiful, clear-running stream at North River, a little more than 200 miles from New York City. At that point there are three sets of rapids that challenge whitewater sports enthusiasts. It is through these stretches of whitewater that the boaters compete in the slalom race on the first day of the Derby. On the second day—Sunday—they compete in the downriver race, or wildwater event. In this event, speed alone is the goal, and the 500 racers are started in small batches. They must paddle against the clock.

Kayaks are the fastest craft, and they appear in the rapids like half-submerged, tiny submarines with the kayakers anchored in the boats, their double-bladed paddles working like windmills as they gain speed and head for the finish line.

With their slim, fiberglass kayaks and their "spray skirts" fitted to themselves and the kayaks, the kayakers know they cannot get water in their boats and sink. But will they tip over? In many cases the answer is "yes." But kayakers know what to do about that.

Next down the Hudson come the covered canoes carrying one or two people. Like the kayakers, the canoeists are usually safe as far as sinking goes, but the two-person canoes are heavier boats than the kayaks and more difficult to maneuver. Some are caught by the current and turned broadside, with the ever-present danger of running into a rock.

With long hours of practice and training behind them, the two-person teams guide their larger canoes down the "chutes." They avoid jutting boulders and punch through standing waves and "haystacks" running the rapids. They emerge dripping wet, but happy.

Last to come are the two-person open canoes, and these are most likely to fill with water or spill boaters into the rapids. When they come down the river on Hudson Derby Day, the spectators, who have gathered just below the rapids, raise thousands of cameras to get

A two-man, closed-deck canoe (C-2) turns over. The boaters wearing life jackets rescue themselves and edge toward shore.

pictures of the action. When an open canoe tips over, the cameras are working at top speed.

The Hudson River Whitewater Derby is only one of hundreds of races run each year in many places throughout the United States. But not all whitewater sportspersons are racers. Thousands of them compete only against the rivers and rapids that can be found from coast to coast—from the West River in Vermont, the Chatooga River in South Carolina, and the Brandywine River in Delaware to the great western rivers, such as the Snake, the Green, and the Colorado.

The sport of whitewater boating began over three quarters of a century ago in Europe. As snow melts each spring in the Alps, the rivers of Germany and Austria become difficult, challenging whitewater runs. Around

/ 3

1900, German sportspersons became fascinated with kayaks, which were "invented" centuries ago by North American Eskimos. The Germans built wood-framed, cloth-covered kayaks for running the rapids. In 1949, the first world championship races were held. Delaware's Brandywine River was the location of the first United States whitewater slalom competition in 1952.

When fiberglass-reinforced plastic was invented, boaters soon figured out that the new material would make good boats. This development really got whitewater sports started in America. The number of whitewater sportspersons is steadily increasing. One major boatbuilding company has nearly doubled the number of boat dealers in its catalogue—from 500 in the early 1970s to almost 1,000.

Nearly every section of the United States has rivers that appeal to whitewater sportspersons. Regional organizations, such as the Appalachian Mountain Club in the Northeast, have listed the streams and rivers that whitewater boaters may use in the area. The rivers are rated according to a system that has developed over the years. There are six classes of rivers rated in order of difficulty (see page 23), so whitewater sportspersons can enjoy the thrills they seek without running the unnecessary risk of going into a river that is too rough for their skills.

A language has been built up, too, as the sport of whitewater boating has grown. Where whitewater boaters gather, terms like "souse hole," "heavy water," "haystack," "chute," "keeper," and many others are used.

The national organization in the United States that

An open canoe enthusiast sticks with her type of boat despite the hazards of a spill.

sets standards and rules for whitewater racing is the American Canoe Association, or ACA. The ACA in turn is a member of the International Canoe Federation, or Federation Internationale de Canoe, which was founded in 1924 under another name. Its present headquarters is in Stockholm, Sweden.

Today, more and more people are learning the thrill and feeling of accomplishment by turning to whitewater for their sport. They are using all kinds of craft. Canoe enthusiasts stick with their time-honored boats. But special dories also are highly prized by a number of whitewater experts in the West who ride the rough waters of the Snake and Colorado Rivers. Trained boaters take beginners on inflated rafts down those and other rivers. Closed-deck canoes for two paddlers are popular all over the country. But the swift, darting kayaks are the most popular craft in use today. And both canoes and kayaks have a long history.

2 / *Where The Boats Come From*

OF THE FOUR types of craft used in the sport of whitewater running, the only modern one is the inflated raft. This was "invented" in the twentieth century. But the other three types—dory, canoe, and kayak—have a long history of use and development.

Dory

Of these three long-established boats, the dory is the most recent. In the nineteenth century, the New England fishing industry began to grow as the nation's population increased. The fishing boats sailed from such ports as Gloucester and Marblehead in Massachusetts and from coastal towns in Maine to fish the Grand Banks off Newfoundland. On the decks of the fishing boats were

"Fog Warning," by Winslow Homer, shows a long-ago fishing dory off the New England coast. Large dories like this now carry parties down whitewater stretches on western rivers. (Courtesy Museum of Fine Arts, Boston)

nets for schools of fish, and there were also stacks of small, one-person boats, called dories. They were "double enders" with pointed bow and stern and a high freeboard (the side of the boat showing above water). They floated lightly on the wave-swept stretches of ocean. The dory was designed for one person to operate, and the operator sat in the middle, or amidships, with the oars. The fishing lines were coiled in the bow. The person's main aim was to catch codfish, for salted-down codfish kept well in the days before refrigeration. The dory was designed to ride rough ocean water. With its high sides, it remained dry inside, and it floated lightly because it rose easily above the waves. It could be rowed backward or forward with the same ease, since both ends were tapered. The dory's high seaworthiness made it an obvious choice for running whitewater, and today it is used on many western rivers where some of the most turbulent whitewater runs.

Canoe

The canoe is one of many types of boats developed by North American Indians. It usually was made of shaved or split green saplings that were tied with deerskin thong and covered with birchbark. The original canoes of the Indians were light and were also "double enders" with pointed bows and sterns. The high curved ends of the typical canoe prevented water from coming in when the craft was taken out on a windy, wave-swept lake. Its lightness made it easy to carry around rapids, which were avoided mainly for fear of damaging the fragile hull of the canoe. It is not known for certain when the Indians developed the canoe, but it was in common use among northern Indian tribes when the first white settlers headed west in the seventeenth century. The light, adaptable boat soon caught the imagination of the settlers themselves. Its maneuverability and lightness have made it a favorite boat for lake and river cruising for over 100 years.

Kayak

The kayak, developed by the Eskimos of Alaska, Canada, and Greenland, is an ingenious invention. Exactly when the kayak was developed will never be known. The Eskimos do not have a written language of their own, and so, no written history. But the small, fast boat's invention may go back several thousands of years. The frame was made of wood, and the ribs, battens

A Greenland Eskimo rides a kayak adapted from the centuries' old design. His "modern" version omits the hand hole in the bow, and is covered with canvas rather than walrus skin.

(running fore and aft), and the heavy gunwale were covered with seal or walrus skin. The hides were sewn together and fastened to the frame with strips of seal skin. The Eskimos who piloted the kayaks wore sealskin parkas, and the skirts of the parkas were drawn tightly around the rim of the small cockpits in which the Eskimos sat. Thus protected from water entering a kayak, an Eskimo could move the light, fast boat in heavy seas without fear of sinking. And, as kayakers do today, the Eskimos used doubled-bladed paddles to maneuver their boats.

Teams of Greenland Eskimos hunted walruses, which they harpooned and towed to shore. In the excitement of the chase and kill, the Eskimos often lost sight of an oncoming wave which often tipped them over. Because they were tied into their boats, the Eskimos developed what whitewater sportspersons today call the "Eskimo roll." By using their paddles and shifting their body weight, the Eskimos learned to turn themselves right side up when their kayaks tipped over.

In the bow and stern of each kayak was a hole for a hand grip or a rope so that the kayak could be dragged on shore. The hand grips allowed an Eskimo to rescue another hunter if he got into serious trouble and his kayak was damaged. When that happened, one of his companions would move the stern of his kayak into place. Then the helpless hunter was able to grab the hand grip hole and save himself. These hand grips, or places for a short bow line, are a part of today's whitewater kayaks. Boaters in trouble because of damaged and sinking kayaks can be hauled out by means of rope loops that they can grab. This form of saving a kayaker is still called by its original name—"Eskimo rescue."

3 / *Whitewater High*

WHITEWATER BOATERS IN the United States have as many opinions about the purpose and goals of their sport as there are boaters. Many of them like to compete in races; others like to find wilderness rivers and enjoy the isolation and thrill of boating down little-known rivers; the goal of still others is to test their skill against the river itself.

Wherever boaters put in their boats and for whatever purposes, it is true that they must compete with the river itself, for that is the essence of whitewater boating. One experienced boater has said that whitewater boating is the last truly amateur sport left in the world—"It's simply you against the river."

But whatever a whitewater boater feels, he or she knows the thrill of hearing the roar of whitewater ahead, the twinge of fear, and the sense of accomplishment when a rapid has been successfully mastered.

A raft full of newcomers to the sport approaches a big wave on California's Stanislaus River. The oarsman is the experienced boater.

The big rivers in the western part of the country such as the Snake and the Colorado, are rivers that only a few years ago were considered too dangerous for boaters. But with the increase in skill and experience, most rivers can now be run by whitewater boaters in whatever craft they may choose. Most western rivers are under the control of the Forest Service Department, and permits are required before boaters can use them. In some cases, the demand to run those rivers is so great that a boater must apply for a permit a year in advance. Experienced local boaters on those rivers grumble about the numbers of boats and rafts that crowd the swift-flowing water.

The big neoprene rafts, manned by persons who

On the mighty Colorado River a loaded raft (towing an empty one) approaches a big wave and avoids a big hole (left).

have run the particular river many times, is the answer to an exciting experience for beginners. In fact, a flourishing business has sprung up along those western rivers, and expeditions stick to strict schedules. For not only is there the thrill of running rapids, but also the joy of camping in true wilderness and hiking up canyons of incredible beauty. The shapes of rock formations and the colors of the canyon walls make the journey an awesome and satisfying experience.

During a recent summer, Joseph Alvord from Kittery, Maine, made such a trip. Here is how he tells about his introduction to the mighty Colorado River in the Grand Canyon.

"I walked a half mile to the rendezvous point. At this time, I'm sacked out under a beautiful green tamarisk bush on the beach waiting for the rafts to appear. The Colorado River (brown as milk chocolate) is about six or eight feet to my right, eddying past, and I'm flat on my back under the tamarisk bush enjoying the shade and a cool breeze. I dozed right off and only woke up when a red ant bit my elbow. Red ants notwithstanding, this is just amazing. Last night in the motel I hadn't even started, and now I am already trying to figure out how I can come out and do this again.

"The rafts showed up about 4:30. The boatmen spent two hours rounding up stray passengers and getting ice from Phantom Ranch for the coolers. I spent the time packing my stuff into two rubberized bags to keep them dry. They are inaccessible during the day, so we each got one white plastic can to keep the things we'll be using during the day—like suntan oil, camera, cup, and extra film. The cans are lashed very securely to the seat so they won't fly off into the river unless some major disaster overtakes us.

"By this time the other five rafts had left (there were six in the expedition) so we were last in line. The stretch below Phantom Ranch is continuous rapids for several miles. They are not strong enough to be dangerous, but rough enough to get us good and wet. The current is very strong and makes standing waves in the river up to six feet high in spots. Below the rapids, the river flattens out and travels smoothly on downriver. But at Horn Creek, we came upon a major rapid. Approaching it was scary in a way. The water is level right up to the edge of the rapid and then drops off sharply. From above, it looks almost like a waterfall. At the top, the water curves smoothly over the edge, and there is a short, exhilarating slide into the waves of the rapid. Then all hell breaks loose. Enormous waves up to ten feet high are the major obstacle. Most of the time, the raft rides right up over them. So we went shooting right through Horn Creek

Rapid in no time at all, and I was almost disappointed. We hardly got wet. The waves are very impressive, though, especially right up close like that."

Joe Alvord's experience with the large rafts explains why beginners who want to try the sport of whitewater boating are put in rafts in the first place. It gives them the thrill and experience of whitewater boating without exposing them to much danger.

But another beginner took a journey down the Snake River in one of the large dories that are the favorite boat among many western-river expedition leaders. In the expedition, the newcomer and his companions were advised of what to do if the dory should turn over. "Above all," their guide and oarsman said, "if the dory turns over, be certain to hang onto it but not on the downstream side. One of the greatest dangers occurs when a boat overturns and the boater is pinned against a rock by the boat itself. Anyone pinned between boat and rock is in a dangerous position."

Having finished giving his instructions, the oarsman and the three newcomers followed the expedition's other two dories out into the current. At first there was some choppy water that splashed the boaters, but it was only Class I or II water and had little effect on the large dory. Then they came to a really heavy rapid—so heavy they could hear its roar from some distance upstream. All three boats pulled into shore, and the new boaters and experts beached the boats and got out to scout the rapids ahead.

Since all the experts had run the rapids many times

/ 15

before, the beginners were surprised by the experienced boaters' careful inspection. It was explained to them that the river changes from day to day—even from hour to hour. It is important, the experts said, to see the heavy rapids before you enter them. They must be carefully studied, and only an expert eye can tell the best route to take on any given day.

The river at that point fell, or dropped quickly, about six feet, and the water divided itself into three distinct falls, or chutes. There were disadvantages in all the chutes, but after the experts had studied the current, the rocks, and the deep holes and huge waves at the bottom of the chutes, they agreed the nearest chute was the least dangerous. To reduce its danger, they agreed that the boat should be rowed hard to the right while it was being carried down the chute, then straight downstream to punch through a big wave. By doing this they would skirt a deep and dangerous hole. If a boat was caught in it, the craft would quickly overturn.

When the beginners got into the dories, they watched the experts for signs of fear and tension. But for the most part the experienced oarsmen hid their emotions. The first dory got safely through, and the oarsman swung it around and brought it to rest in an eddy to one side of the turbulent water. From there he could watch the other boats make the run. He would also be on hand in case help was needed. The second boat got safely through. But the third boat did not move far enough to the right, and it went straight into the hole, or "keeper," as such turbulence is called. The oarsman lost an oar, the boat flipped over, and the new boaters found themselves underneath the dory which was churning around in the keeper. They had been told what to do in case they came up underneath the boat. They were to hold onto the boat no matter what happened, and haul themselves to the upstream side. This they did. Then they ducked out from beneath the dory, held afloat by their life jackets, and clung to the overturned boat.

The river was kind to them that day. While they were struggling out from beneath the boat, the heavy current swept them safely out of the hole. They soon found themselves downstream, but still in whitewater. The expert was there, too, and he hauled the bowline aft and hooked it around an oarlock. Then he threw the line over the upturned bottom of the boat and used it to haul himself onto it. By leaning hard upstream, he was trying to turn the boat right side up while it bounced and swept through the rapids. Two of the beginners went to his aid.

Slowly, so slowly they could scarcely see it happening, the boat began to be a help rather than a hindrance. Finally, the boat turned right side up in the water, although it was filled with water. The men and the one woman passenger scrambled in and began bailing out the water as fast as they could. Those in the boat that had stood by to help them offered an oar to replace the one that had been lost when the dory capsized. A man in the rescue boat hurled the oar like a harpoon, and the oarsman in the other boat caught it. He immediately put oars into the oarlocks, sat down, and began once more to direct the boat in the heavy water.

He began rowing just in time. The dory hit another rapid below the first big one. But by this time, the passengers had bailed out the boat. It regained its buoyancy, and the party was swept downriver toward their next stopping place. They were safe.

Everyone had been afraid. Everyone had been caught by the heavy whitewater. But everyone had worked to bring the boat safely through the rapids. Although everyone was soaking wet, they had had a good time.

When kayaks or canoes run the big western rivers, the expedition usually consists of one or two rafts to carry camping equipment and to act as a "mother hen" to a brood of adventurous kayakers and canoeists. On one such expedition on the Colorado, six kayakers and canoeists, accompanied by two rafts, made a ten-day journey. The kayaks and canoes shot turbulent rapids, such as the Unkar, Sockdolager, Horn, Granite, Crystal, and Hermit. All the canoeists and kayakers were experts. All experienced fear. All but one turned over at least once. All made it safely through the heaviest whitewater the country has to offer.

One of the kayakers told of seeing his buddy trying to handle a wave. He noticed the "ordinarily poker-faced" man's expression change from "fright to sheer terror" as his kayak plummeted down a twenty-foot wave to the turbulence below.

As the seasons pass, more and more whitewater boaters are trying their skill and courage on rapids across the country. In a kayak, it is only one person against the

A skilled kayaker heads for a froth chute on California's American River. Only recently have kayakers been allowed on the big western rivers.

river. But with friends and other whitewater boaters, the person has a comradeship and a closeness found only among groups that face and solve troublesome problems together.

Like participants in all sports, whitewater boaters share their fears, their accomplishments, and, whenever possible, their information and skills. They find it an exciting sport—one that allows them to test themselves against the ever-flowing, ever-turbulent whitewater from South Carolina to Oregon. There may be spills, cold dunkings, and long walks, but the boaters will be unable to resist the lure of whitewater. Each will wonder whether he or she can handle the roaring rapids that lie just ahead.

/ 19

4 / *Where Whitewater Runs*

IN MOST OF the United States, whitewater boating is a seasonal sport, not because boaters don't like to run rapids all year long, but because the rivers themselves change with the seasons and at certain times make whitewater sport impossible.

Rivers everywhere depend on water depth from the land above them. When winter snows melt, rivers take the runoff, and the rivers broaden and deepen. During this time of year, rivers in the Northeast and North Middlewest can be used by whitewater sportsmen. When the snow-melt has gone, the rivers in many parts of the country become too shallow for whitewater boating.

Part of this is due to the land and part of it is due to the work of people. If the upland forests above a river have been cut over, the land will not absorb much water or be able to hold it. When snow melts there, it runs off quickly. The rivers rise fast, but they shallow out equally fast.

The same thing is true after heavy rains. The water runs off quickly, giving a day or two of good boating before the river gets too shallow again.

If the land above the river source is undisturbed and the ancient forests remain, a great deal more water is absorbed by the ground because it is protected by trees. The trees act like a sponge that holds water, releasing it slowly and steadily to feed the river below. In the far western states, the watersheds of many rivers are like this, and the rivers there can be run by whitewater boaters much of the year. This is true, also, in Canada and in northern Maine.

In the southern and mid-Atlantic states, the best whitewater running comes during the winter. Whitewater enthusiasts there have to put up with the cold when boating.

Strength of Flowing Water

No one takes up the sport of whitewater boating without quickly learning to respect the flowing water. One beginner, who was planning to run the whitewater of the Snake River with an experienced boater, studied the "chute," or narrow waterfall, down which his dory was to go. The swift, plunging, unstoppable water made him wonder whether he was doing the right thing. He later calculated that 30,000 cubic feet of water was going

A relatively placid stretch of water on the Eel River in California is classed between II and III by whitewater experts.

down the chute every second, and each cubic foot weighed 62.4 pounds. That is 936 tons of water every second.

A boat or raft, overturned and pinned against a rock, may be pushed by the water against the rock with such force that no amount of pulling with a rope will free it. In such a case, the only thing whitewater boaters can do is wait for the river to go down before they are able to rescue their craft.

The International Canoe Federation has classified whitewater rivers in terms of their strength and turbulence. All whitewater sportspersons pay heed to the ratings. A number of things come into the classification system: the volume of water flowing; the slope of the river bed or how fast it is going "downhill"; the course of the river (a river with many bends and turns is more difficult to navigate); and how rugged and rocky the river bed is.

Here are the ICF's classifications:

I   Few waves of any kind, no sharp bends, no obstructions.

II   More waves (up to a foot high), clear, and wide-coursed; current faster than in I.

III   Many waves up to three feet in height, clear passages through rapids. If narrow, has eddies, protruding rocks. Not for beginners.

IV   Large waves; irregular, fast currents; boiling eddies. Must be inspected (from the river bank) before trying it.

V   Long, powerful rapids with pounding waves, very steep gradient of river bed, many obstructions. Must be carefully inspected first. Only for the very expert.

VI   Almost completely unnavigable with high waves, shifting currents, and many obstructions. No one should try it.

If a whitewater expert is on a strange river and sees evidence of whitewater ahead, the boater paddles to the shore, drags the boat up, and walks downstream along the bank to inspect the rapids. As an expert, he or she can study the rapids and note the eddies, souse holes, rollers, and haystacks. There may be two or three "chutes," where water pours down a steep slope between two or more rocks or over ledges. The person judges them and chooses the best chute to try. Then the person goes back to the boats, prepares for the swift, exciting journey, and shoves off.

Boil

While studying the river, the expert might have noted quite a number of things, each of which has its own name. The boater might have seen a "boil," an upswelling of water that forms a bump. Beneath the water's surface there is an obstruction over which the water must flow. Sometimes there is enough water flowing over it so a shallow-floating raft can get over. A canoe or a dory might hit that obstruction on the upstream face and immediately might be pinned there by the force of the flowing water.

Haystack

A boater might see what is called a "haystack," a short stationary or standing wave. It is caused by fast-running water flowing downward between two rocks. At the bottom of the falls, the water spouts upward almost vertically, forming the wave. The wave remains where it is; if it cannot be avoided, the boat has to go through it. In a kayak this means a dunking. In an open canoe it means a dunking and some water in the boat.

Eddy

A rock jutting above the surface forces the flowing water to go around it. When it flows around the

A kayak goes over a ledge into a wave on the Swift River in New Hampshire.

downstream side of the rock, it curves in behind the rock, where there is a current moving upstream. Such an "eddy" can provide a resting place for a weary kayaker or canoeist. Tucked into an eddy downstream of a rock, the boat is in motionless water as far as current is concerned. But not all eddies are nice to be in. Some have strong upward or swirling currents that can overturn a boat. Instead of resting, the boater has to constantly work with a paddle to stay upright.

Keeper, hole, and stopper

If swift water flows over a ledge, a low dam, or a weir, the water all across the river plunges down and then rises a few feet below the ledge or dam to form long-standing waves. A souse hole is the same thing, but does not stretch across the river. The wave is the result of the water falling, forming a trough, then "bouncing" up. The words used to describe this potentially dangerous flow of water differ in a number of areas of the country. But "keeper" is perhaps the most accurate word because the trough in front of the wave can completely stop a whitewater boat or raft. Not only is a keeper hard to get out of; it also can cause a wreck.

When the water flows over a ledge or dam, it splits into two currents. The water near the bottom of the river flows downstream, forming a deep but strong current. The water near the surface curls back on itself, forming a frothy mixture of air and water. It tumbles over and over like clothes in a clothes dryer. The downstream portion forms a curling, lashing wave.

One whitewater boater described a keeper as "a place that could re-cycle a canoe or a kayak or a raft as well as the people in the canoe or raft." People who are dumped into a keeper may want to get out of their life jackets to save their lives, for this churning, surface water rolls boats and their occupants over and over, without letting go of them. Experienced whitewater sportspersons have found that to escape a keeper, they must often abandon their boats, shed their life jackets, and dive below the frothy, boiling surface to reach the deep flowing current that will take them underneath the wave and downstream to quieter, safer water.

All expert whitewater boaters avoid keepers or stoppers whenever possible. When it is impossible to avoid them, they gain as much speed as possible before reaching them and enter the "hole" head on. If a boat turns broadside to the current, it will be caught and roll endlessly in the surface maelstrom. But with speed and proper alignment, a boat can make it through a keeper and proceed on its way. Such a maneuver is called "punching through" a wave.

Whitewater experts would never enter such rough water alone. They would be certain to have some of their friends on a nearby bank with ropes to throw their way in the event they are caught in the swirling water. And the more experienced the whitewater boaters are, the more cautious they become in such circumstances. They know and respect the huge forces at work in the flowing rivers. Many of them carry throw ropes in case they get in trouble.

5 / Today's Whitewater Craft

THE BOATS THAT whitewater buffs use come in many shapes and sizes—from inner tubes to rafts and large double-ended, flat-bottomed dories. No serious whitewater person uses an inner tube, of course, but there are rivers where mild, harmless rapids provide people with a lot of bobbing around as they float among the riffles and small waves.

There are four basic types of "boats" in use today. Each has its special use, and each has its group of faithful followers who believe their type of boat is the best. Modern technology has helped in the design and building of all types of today's boats. Without the synthetic fibers and binding resins that are used now, there would be a lot less whitewater activity.

Three modern whitewater boats ride placidly in flatwater. Left to right: Two-man, closed-deck canoe (C-2); one-man, closed-deck canoe (C-1); one-man kayak (K-1).

Inflatable Raft

Rafts used in whitewater boating are not the thin-skinned, small rafts seen at beaches or swimming pools. Whitewater rafts are capable of holding as many as eight people, although four-person rafts are more common and less expensive. Rafts have two or more airtight "compartments" that give them great buoyancy. They are made of tough, plastic fabric that can withstand snagging on subsurface rocks or logs without springing a leak. They are fitted with oarlocks, and many can be run by an outboard motor attached to one end.

Rafts have been used in the roughest water in the country. Today there are many experienced commercial

/ 29

groups that regularly offer tours for beginners on the western rivers. The beginners' efforts are usually restricted to helping to bail out the raft if it ships water. The guiding and rowing is left to the rafts' owners who are familiar with the rivers and skilled in maneuvering the large, bulky rafts.

Since even the biggest rafts ride high in the water, they can scoot over boulders that ordinarily would snag a boat that rides lower in the water.

Dory

The river dories used today are larger than the original fishing dories. They hold five or more people, but are maneuvered by the one most skilled at handling the two eight-foot oars in the oarlocks amidships. Many of the experienced boaters who run western-river tours swear by their dories which they believe are the best passenger craft for whitewater journeys.

Open Canoe

The open canoe, usually paddled by two persons, has been used for many years for flat-water cruising and non-turbulent downriver journeys. Not many years ago, canoes were made of wood frames covered with waterproof canvas. Later, they were made entirely of laminated strips of wood. Today, most canoes are made either

Walley Williams of Belmont, Massachusetts, single-handedly handles an aluminum open canoe while taking a student into whitewater. Open canoes are usually manned by two people.

of aluminum or fiberglass. Boaters who love open canoes swear by their style of boat and tend to look at all other whitewater craft as less worthy.

Open canoes are limited, however, in the amount of heavy whitewater they can successfully face. Two persons operating an open canoe in whitewater must be highly skilled and work closely as a team. It takes practice and co-ordination to navigate even moderate whitewater turbulence without swamping a canoe or flipping over. Class III rivers are often defined as the top limit for an open canoe.

Even though the open canoe was never meant to run rapids, the stubbornness of canoeists makes them try to

/ 31

compete against more waterproof, maneuverable craft. There are few races or competitions involving open canoes that do not see many contestants upending in whitewater or swamping and filling below some chute.

Closed-deck Canoe

Since so many open canoes get swamped in turbulent water, it seems obvious that a waterproof deck should be added to the canoe, and this is exactly what has been done. Closed-deck canoes for one or two persons can be seen on many stretches of whitewater. In fact, the one-person, closed-deck canoe resembles the kayak. It can most easily be spotted because the person paddling is in a kneeling position; the kayak paddler is seated. The canoeist's paddle is single-bladed, a typical canoe paddle.

The one-person canoe is the second fastest whitewater boat in use (second only to the kayak). The two-person, closed-deck canoe, when handled by experts in whitewater, is definitely the boat to watch. The coordination and skill of a good two-person crew guiding their craft down river is quite a sight.

Kayak

When most people today think of whitewater racing, they think of kayaks. These fast, highly maneuverable boats have caught the attention of most televi-

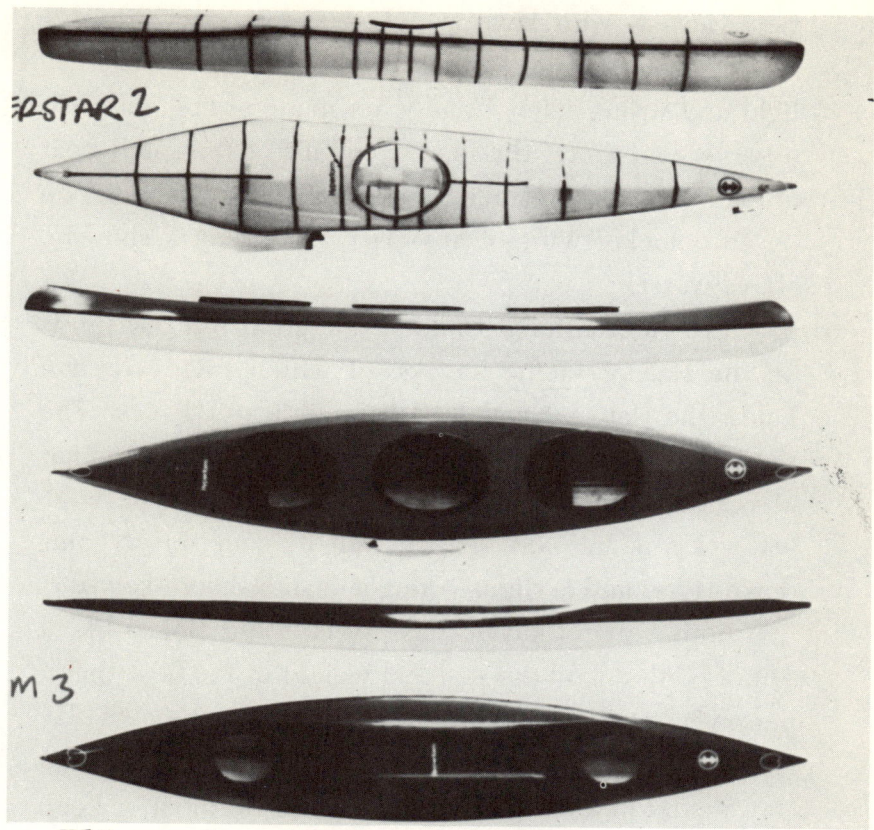

Whitewater boats come in many designs. Here, from top to bottom, are a one-man, downriver (wildwater racing), closed-deck canoe (C-1); a two-man, touring, closed-deck canoe with a center compartment for camping gear; a two-man, closed-deck slalom canoe (C-2).

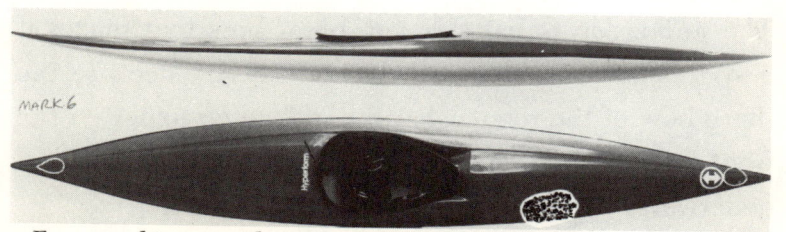

Fastest whitewater boats are one-man kayaks. This is a slalom-racing K-1.

/ 33

sion viewers who have watched slalom or wildwater races down frothing rivers. Today's racing kayaks are light and strong. They usually are made of fiberglass. To observers on shore, the lone occupant of the small boat often appears to be sinking, and the kayaker may sweep by an onlooker without any part of the kayak showing above water.

The International Canoe Federation has put limits on the size of racing kayaks, of which there are two kinds: the slalom kayak and the wildwater kayak. The slalom kayak is shorter than the wildwater kayak, and has a rounded hull for quick, easy maneuvering. The wildwater kayak has a V-shaped hull to gain speed going down-river, and is slightly longer than a slalom kayak.

Both types of kayaks have to be fitted almost like a suit of clothes, and the size and weight of the boat that a person purchases is determined by the buyer's own size and weight.

Slalom kayaks, without keels to guide them or keep them upright, often skid and slip around on the water's surface until the kayaker develops more skill and a "feel" for the boat. The maneuverability of kayaks is an astonishing thing to watch, and it is little wonder that a surfing kayak has been developed to ride ocean waves. The surfing kayak has a broad, blunt bow that makes it easy to spot. The blunt bow was necessary because the sharp bow of the regular kayak tends to go under on the front of a wave and give the "surfyaker" a total underwater experience as the wave passes over.

Maneuvering a Kayak

An expert kayaker makes handling a kayak look easy. But these little boats are very sensitive to slight shifts of weight and the changing forces of river currents on their sides. A person riding in a kayak is in more ways than one "wearing the boat." The kayaker is seated in a small cockpit; his or her feet are pressed firmly on the foot braces, with knees tight against the knee braces. The curved sides of the seat act as hip braces. The kayaker is able to exert force on the craft with feet, knees, and hips.

Double-bladed paddles are used exclusively with kayaks. The paddles have blades set at right angles to one another. With the paddle as a propeller, lever, and rudder, the kayaker and the kayak ride the whitewater like a duck—turning, darting swiftly across the surface and resting in an eddy.

The kayaker wears a spray skirt that is fitted to the out-curling rim of the cockpit. This makes the kayak almost waterproof.

With spray skirt in place, a kayaker can lean to one side or another without water entering the kayak. If the boat churns through a standing wave or haystack, the entire kayak may disappear; all a spectator can see is the head and shoulders of the kayaker. Beyond the wave, however, the kayak will bob to the surface. The kayaker's paddle continues to drive the boat and its pilot forward, and they are soon out of sight.

Beginners are often surprised at how quickly a kayak

A skilled kayaker uses a Duffek brace to turn his kayak quickly.

overturns. If the kayak is moving from the almost motionless water of an eddy into a fast, downstream current, the current can strike the bow and flip the kayak over in the wink of an eye. It has been described as exactly the same feeling as having a rug suddenly pulled out from under you.

With their double-bladed paddles, experienced kayakers anticipate all the forces of a river. By driving their blades in the water, they can move straight forward easily by using the forward stroke; they can "back up" by using the back stroke. They also can lean to one side to reduce the force of a side current on the hull of the kayak.

Only in the last few years have certain paddle strokes been developed that give the kayak its great maneuverability. The man who invented the most important new stroke is Milovan Duffek, a Czechoslovakian kayaker. When he showed his new stroke at a World

Championship meet in the 1950s, it immediately caught on. When he went fast downriver and wanted to turn, he leaned slightly in the direction he wanted to go, reached out with his paddle as far away from the kayak as possible, and put the blade into the water. The force of the water on the blade spun the boat around in a quick turn, and the kayaker's body, extended arms, and paddle acted as levers to increase the effect of the force on the blade.

In addition to turning the kayak and driving it forward or backward, the paddle is used also to keep the kayak from turning over when sudden currents, waves, and swirls threaten to capsize the boat. Such strokes are called "braces." They are used separately or combined with driving strokes and turning strokes.

In a brace, the paddle acts as an outrigger to keep the kayak upright. This is especially true of a high brace, where the kayaker extends the paddle as far out from the kayak's side as possible before dipping the paddle blade into the current. The blade is held vertically. In this position the kayak is kept from rolling over. From this brace position, the kayaker can convert the motion quickly into a driving stroke and move ahead.

Many of these developments in maneuvering kayaks have been used only for a few years. But it is because of them that the kayak has become so popular.

The expert kayaker will move this craft so quickly and so smoothly along a river course or through the racing slalom gates that spectators often miss most of the paddle techniques.

6 / Training, Safety, and Equipment

No MATTER WHAT kind of boat a whitewater sportsbuff uses, the participant is going to be dunked in the water many times. Large rafts are the least likely to overturn, but in very rough rapids, even large rafts will overturn and spill the crew into the rapids.

Of all the types of boats, the open canoe is the most likely to overturn or fill with water. Closed-deck canoes prevent sudden swampings, and the almost waterproof kayaks take to dunking like ducks. But no kayaker should try out whitewater without a great deal of training and practice.

During the winter months, more and more indoor swimming pools are being used by boaters. There they can practice maneuvering their boats, and can learn how to recover from a spill when they do turn over.

Eskimo Roll

When the Eskimos developed kayaks, they had the same problem about turning over that whitewater kayakers do today. And they did something about it. They learned how to use their paddles and their bodies to right themselves and go on about their business of fishing or hunting. Today's expert kayakers can do this more gracefully perhaps, but they do it essentially the way Eskimos did many years ago.

Kayakers, of course, are tucked into their kayaks with their feet on braces, their knees fitted in pocket knee braces on the underside of the kayaks' "decks," and they are firmly wedged in their seats. They can thus exert force on the hulls of the kayaks by twisting their hips and driving hard with their paddles. Their spray skirts prevent water from flooding the kayaks.

When they find themselves upside down, with their heads underwater, beginning kayakers may panic and forget what they are supposed to do. They should leave the kayaks and make what is called "wet exits." In other words, they should release the spray skirts from the edges of the cockpit, take their knees from the knee braces, and push themselves out of the kayak. They should also hold on to their paddles as they surface. If kayakers are not wearing nose plugs, they should exhale air while upside down in order to keep water from entering their noses. Once they are on top of the water, they should work their way to the bows or sterns of the kayaks, where there are loops of rope. Holding the "grabloop" and the

The Eskimo Roll: It is commonplace for kayaks and C-1's to tip over. Whitewater boater Walley Williams of Belmont, Massachusetts, plays in a hole (1) tips over, (2) goes into an Eskimo Roll, and (3) comes upright, even though his spray skirt parted from his C-1 canoe.

paddle in one hand, the kayaker can then begin to swim to shore without losing the kayak downstream.

Once beginning kayakers overcome the panic of being upside down in the water, they can learn to use the Eskimo roll to recover from a spill. Of course, they must first practice in quiet water, with someone standing by to assist, before they set out in whitewater. But many kayakers, who have learned how to right themselves by using the Eskimo roll in a swimming pool or a quiet pond, find that the panic clings to them when they are actually in whitewater. It may take a long time before that panic goes away for good.

When they have learned the Eskimo roll and used it in a fast-flowing river, kayakers have learned the most valuable survival maneuver in kayaking.

One-person, closed-deck canoes (C-1's) can also use the Eskimo roll. Well co-ordinated teams, paddling a two-person closed-deck canoe, can also return to an upright position using the roll. But a two-person roll requires expert timing and a good deal of strength, since the longer, heavier canoes are harder to turn right side up.

Most intructors in the handling of whitewater craft insist that beginners learn how to roll upright or get out of overturned boats before they learn anything else. One expert who has trained many kayakers insists that the first thing his students learn is to get out of, or turn upright, an overturned kayak. Then, and only then, does he teach them the forward or driving stroke and the other strokes needed to maneuver the small, light craft.

/ 41

Eskimo Rescue

All trained boaters know that no person should be alone in whitewater. The chances of overturning are too great, and if overturned boaters are in the rocky part of a river, they can be stunned and unable to help themselves. If they can flip upright again, using the Eskimo roll, they will be all right. But if they cannot do the Eskimo roll, another kayaker can help them turn right side up. The assisting kayak is moved so its stern is within reach of the overturned kayakers' hands. The upside-down kayakers can reach the grabloop on the bow of the helping kayak and use it to pull themselves upright.

As the sport of whitewater boating grows, more and more clinics and schools are being started to train boaters. One such clinic is Camp Mondamin in the mountainous area of North Carolina, near the small town of Tuxedo. The camp's owners bring experts from all over the country to teach would-be boaters everything they must know to handle whitewater—from the kinds of boats to buy to reading a river and righting a boat. The canoe clinic, as it is known, is near whitewater rivers of different degrees of difficulty. The course lasts ten days during which a boater is trained to run a river without danger.

The first thing the instructors do is to find out whether the students can swim—and swim they must in order to go on from there. Little by little, the difficulties are increased. When the students are good enough, they are taken to a stretch of the nearby Chatooga River to

Outfitted whitewater boaters—wearing helmets, life jackets, wet suits, and spray skirts—are ready to ride.

run some really rough rapids—rapids that saw film action in the movie "Deliverance" several years ago. When they graduate, the students are able to run whitewater successfully.

Equipment

Whitewater canoeists and kayakers need a lot more than boats and paddles to enjoy their sport. Foremost among the things they must have are life jackets. They are required gear, and very nearly all the bad accidents that have occurred in this sport have come from the failure to wear life jackets. Since 1973, the U.S. Coast Guard, under the Department of Transportation, has

/ 43

Whitewater helmets have outer shells with large drainage holes suspended on adjustable harnesses that fit the head. The combined shell and harness increase safety for the wearer.

required that all occupants of boats under sixteen feet in length be supplied with life jackets.

The best jacket for whitewater boating is light in weight, but also tough enough to withstand being scraped against rocks. It also is designed to support the head and shoulders of the wearer, keeping the person's head out of water. Because expert whitewater boaters know they have to be able to paddle freely and turn the upper part of their bodies, they want a jacket that fits snugly and is zippered or strapped in front. They do not use bulky life jackets, with heavy collars, even though they are less expensive.

When the sport of whitewater boating was new, boaters got equipment wherever they could find it. They knew they needed helmets to protect their heads when they tipped over, but at first, all they could find were hockey helmets or bike-racers' helmets. Now, of course, special helmets for whitewater boating are made—and worn by canoeists and kayakers alike.

In many parts of the country, whitewater boating begins in late spring. In the North, the water is still very cold in the spring. In the South, the best whitewater

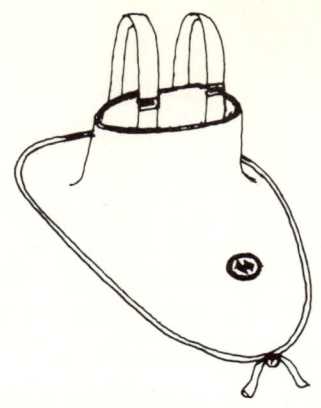

Spray skirts prevent water from entering the cockpit of a closed-deck boat. The skirt is drawn tightly around the rim of the cockpit to waterproof the boat.

boating time is in the winter, but even in many of the southern states, the waters off the mountains are cold. To protect themselves against the cold water, the boaters wear special "wet suits" of neoprene rubber. These suits, developed for ocean divers, are valued by whitewater boaters. The reason why is simple. If the human body is suddenly dunked in very cold water, the shock to the nervous system is immediate. By wearing a wet suit of the proper weight, a boater can easily withstand the shock of cold water, and some wet-suit wearers even claim that such a dunking is pleasant. As further protection against cold, experts suggest gloves for cold weather, as well as lightweight nylon jackets. The boaters' hands will stay sensitive and be able to operate, and their arms and shoulders will be safe from chilling winds.

Kayakers have another piece of equipment to keep them snug and warm—the spray skirt. Tucked into their kayaks, they spread out the spray skirts and fit the edges of them around the lips, or coamings, of the cockpits. They draw them tight with drawstrings so that no water can enter the boats, and even the dripping water from the paddles won't get their laps wet. With the spray skirts in place, kayakers keep the lower parts of their bodies warm inside the dry hulls of their small boats. Of course, all spray skirts have release cords which are placed within reach of the kayakers—either in front or to one side of the cockpits. If a kayak tips over and the kayaker decides to get out of the kayak, the person's first move is to release the spray skirt by pulling the release cord.

If a canoeist or kayaker has all the proper equipment, he or she can safely and comfortably challenge the next stretch of whitewater without worrying about what will happen in a spill—even in the coldest water.

Boaters' Precautions

Boaters should always work in pairs or groups. Even when kayakers are racing, they are started in groups. It is a hard rule of whitewater boating that any boater who sees a person in trouble in the water will offer help—even if the trouble occurs in the middle of a race.

In very rough water, the most experienced boater often starts out first. When the boater is safely through the rapids, he or she finds an eddy, then turns and waits for the next boat to come through. In this way, the first boater through the rapids can lend a helping hand if the following boats upset and need help.

Boaters often have friends stationed along the shore as an extra precaution. The supporting person or group has ropes that can be thrown to anyone in trouble.

Many people who have taken up the sport are thankful that such help is usually at hand, as it was for one inexperienced kayaker on a wild river in western Pennsylvania. When he and his friend were planning a run through some heavy whitewater, they met an expert kayaker, a young woman who had run those rapids many times. The two young men set out and promptly got into a hole where they both capsized. One young man, unsure of the Eskimo roll, tried to execute a wet exit while tumbling around in the churning water. His life preserver popped him to the surface just as the current took him into another tumbling wave. While he was gasping for air and totally confused, he saw the girl edging her kayak toward him for an Eskimo rescue. He grasped the grab-loop of her kayak and got safely ashore.

7 / *Racing*

FOR MANY YEARS, flatwater canoe racing has been an Olympic Games event. The term "flatwater" means just that: no rapids, no turbulence, smooth paddling. But European interest in whitewater canoeing and kayaking as a sport was on the increase, and by 1972 the Olympic Games Committee included a whitewater slalom event that attracted a lot of attention.

Today there are two types of whitewater racing and five classes of boats in which racers may qualify under the regulations of the International Canoe Federation.

The two types of racing are wildwater and slalom. The classes of boats recognized by the ICF are: 1) the K-1, or one-man kayak; 2) the K-1W, a one-woman kayak; 3) the C-1, a one-man canoe with a closed deck; 4) the C-2, a two-man, closed-deck canoe; and 5) the C-2M, a closed-deck canoe with a man and a woman operating it.

A slalom kayak (K-1) maneuvers through a gate in a slalom race.

While these are the official ICF classes, various national and regional organizations permit other types of boats to enter whitewater racing meets. Two women, for example, may operate a C-2 in meets; and one woman might paddle a C-1, since the exclusion of women from this sport has almost entirely disappeared. In some parts of the United States, canoe lovers even go into heavy whitewater races in open canoes. This often leads to a lot of swamped canoes and what are called "DF's" and "FW's," or "Didn't Finish" and "Finished Walking."

In the United States, the American Canoe Association is the official organization that lists local and regional competitions and the U.S. National Championships each year. A recent issue of *Canoe,* the ACA's official publication, listed over 120 whitewater meets scheduled to take place from March through November. These were to take place throughout the country—from Alabama to Washington and from California to Maine. In addition, there were listings of twenty-three international competitions, including the World Championship meet in Spittal, Austria.

Whitewater racers take these meets and the championships every bit as seriously as athletes in any other world-competitive sport. Internationally known kayaker and slalom-racer Norbert Sattler, for example, began competing in whitewater slalom racing in his native Austria when he was thirteen. He has been at it ever since. He has won the Austrian National Championship and the silver medal in the Olympic competition. Sattler represents the dedication some whitewater kayakers have. He lifts weights, bicycles, and gets as many as three workouts every day on whitewater slalom courses.

In addition to the listed competitions, both national and international, canoe and kayak organizations all over the country put on their own competitions throughout the whitewater season. Whitewater sportspersons are incurably fascinated by the sight and sound of a swift-flowing river and the roar of rapids. With wet suits, helmets, and life jackets, they launch their kayaks and canoes and move out into the current to begin another contest between themselves and the whitewater ahead.

Before a race, experienced whitewater boaters make every effort to become acquainted with the river and its rapids. In some competitions, practice is allowed before the start of an actual race. In such a case, the river will be alive with canoeists or kayakers practicing the course. They will memorize the turns, the eddies, the location of the chutes, and particularly dangerous souse holes. And even though a kayaker has run that particular river before, the racer will study it as thoroughly as a newcomer because changing water levels (which occur from day to day) can make a familiar route completely different from one day to the next.

If free practice is not allowed, competitors might be seen stalking the banks on both sides of the river long before the race begins. Many will have notebooks and pencils in hand, as they study every small action of the course. It is only by doing this that racers can know how to attack the river, where the troubles may lie, and where they can gain a few seconds' advantage over their rivals.

Wildwater Race

Wildwater races are simple, straightforward competitions to see who can complete the course in the shortest time. The usual length of the course is between three and sixteen miles. If it is a long course, the racers know they will have to conserve their strength and try to make the river do as much work for them as possible. The stamina required for such a race is great. Even kayakers in excellent condition know that their best strength is no match for the force of the river. This means that when they start downstream, a great part of their effort will be to conserve their strength.

On a long course, the speed will be slower than on a short one because each racer conserves his or her strength against the trial ahead. The racers try to avoid eddies that will slow them, and holes that might upset their craft. They remember the channels of water that are moving the fastest, and they head for them. If they have done their preliminary scouting accurately, they will recognize every rock, every bend, and every eddy and hole they meet.

When the finish line comes in sight, all the racers go into a frenzied sprint, throwing every ounce of muscle they have into their stroking. They know that a second or two cut off their time can easily mean the difference between a winning trophy and a losing place.

Slalom Race

Slalom racing is the most difficult race of all. Although several classes of boats undertake the slalom, the K-1 kayak is best suited for the maneuvering that makes a winner.

A slalom course is not so long as a wildwater run. The International Canoe Federation's requirements are that it be not more than 800 meters (875 yards or about one half of a mile long). In this distance on fast-running, turbulent water, there are from twelve to thirty "gates" through which the racers must pass.

A slalom gate consists of two poles that are hung vertically by wires over the river a few feet apart. The lower ends of the poles hang just above the water's surface.

Depending on the river and the difficulty of the

Two-man slalom canoes require great teamwork. Here, one approaches the first of two closely-spaced gates.

race, the gates may be in the center of the current, behind rocks, in an eddy, or on the edge of an eddy. Racers have to move their boats through each gate to get downstream in the least possible time.

But this is not all. The gates are marked, and they may be in any one of three categories. The easiest is the downstream gate, which the racer goes through and then heads as fast as possible downstream toward the next gate. The second category is the upstream gate. The racer must go downstream of the gate outside it, turn, and paddle upstream while passing between the poles. The third and most difficult category is the reverse gate. To pass through it correctly, the racer must turn the boat quickly just upstream of the gate and pass through it, stern first, with the bow pointed upstream.

As in any other race, of course, time is important. But in slalom, skill in running the rapids and maneuvering the boat actually count more than time. If a slalom racer's boat touches one of the poles, the racer is penalized ten seconds. If the participant touches both poles, he or she gets a twenty-second penalty, and if the racer misses the gate altogether, fifty seconds is added to the boater's time.

According to experts, the whitewater slalom has done more to improve the sport than anything else. As a result, kayak design has improved. With more racers concentrating on executing the "perfect slalom," new paddle techniques have become common skills for experienced kayakers.

No two slalom courses are the same. Except for the length requirements and the number of gates to pass through, slalom courses differ as widely as the rivers they are laid out on. These rivers may be of any difficulty between Class II and Class IV.

Even on the same stretch of the same river, courses can differ, depending on where the gates are placed and what the water level is during a race.

Practice for Slalom Racing

Contenders for national and international standing in whitewater racing train as extensively for the slalom events as contenders in any other sport. They exercise in a variety of ways to increase their muscular coordination and endurance. In the off-season, when rivers are frozen or too low to boat on, whitewater enthusiasts practice in swimming pools.

One of the best training maneuvers in a pool, in a pond, or on a quiet river is called the "English Gate."

Those who practice it faithfully do very well when they enter slalom competition the next season.

The English Gate consists of two poles, set a yard apart, over a pool or pond. The kayaker first goes forward through the gate, makes a right turn, and goes back through the gate from the other side. He or she then makes a left about turn and goes through the gate again.

The kayaker immediately paddles backward outside one of the poles. When he or she reaches the other side of the gate, he or she does an Eskimo roll and goes forward diagonally through the gates. Then the boater paddles backward on the outside of the other pole, does another Eskimo roll, and goes forward diagonally through the gate again.

The next maneuver is to paddle backward, outside, past the left pole, make a reverse turn and go stern-first through the gate, and make another reverse turn and go back through the gate again.

The fourth step is to go forward outside the right-hand pole, do an Eskimo roll, and go backward diagonally through the gate. The kayaker then goes forward outside of the left-hand pole, does an Eskimo roll in the opposite direction of the one just completed, and paddles backward through the gate diagonally to the finish point.

This rigorous and complex practice-run has been accomplished by experts in less than a minute. Not-so-expert kayakers can complete the exercise in ninety to 100 seconds.

The effectiveness of practicing the English gate in the offseason was proved not long ago by a small group of kayakers in training. They were beginners. When the racing season started, several of them placed very near the top of the list in the slalom competitions they entered.

Future of Racing

It is safe to say that slalom racing and any other competition that people may invent in the future will be practiced as long as whitewater sport remains. Team races, marathons, relays, and any number of variations will attract boaters. Most of such racing is designed to increase the skill of kayakers and canoeists. But besides all the races, there is the competitors' true opponent: the river. With increased skill, boaters will be safer and happier, and they also will have more thrills while learning to ride the whitewater.